Georgia, My State
Habitats

Marsh and Swamp

by Doraine Bennett

STATE
STANDARDS
PUBLISHING LLC ®

Your State • Your Standards • Your Grade Level

Dear Educators, Librarians and Parents . . .

Thank you for choosing the *"Georgia, My State"* Series! We have designed this series to support the Georgia Department of Education's Georgia Performance Standards for elementary level Georgia studies. Each book in the series has been written at appropriate grade level as measured by the ATOS Readability Formula for Books (Accelerated Reader), the Lexile Framework for Reading, and the Fountas & Pinnell Benchmark Assessment System for Guided Reading. Photographs and/or illustrations, captions, and other design elements have been included to provide supportive visual messaging to enhance text comprehension. Glossary and Word Index sections introduce key new words and help young readers develop skills in locating and combining information.

We wish you all success in using the *"Georgia, My State"* Series to meet your student or child's learning needs. For additional sources of information, see www.georgiaencyclopedia.org.

Jill Ward, President

Publisher
State Standards Publishing, LLC
1788 Quail Hollow
Hamilton, GA 31811
USA
1.866.740.3056
www.statestandardspublishing.com

Library of Congress Cataloging-in-Publication Data
Bennett, Doraine, 1953-
  Marsh and Swamp / by Doraine Bennett.
      p. cm. -- (Georgia, my state. Habitats)
  Includes index.
  ISBN-13: 978-1-935077-36-7 (hardcover)
  ISBN-10: 1-935077-36-8 (hardcover)
  ISBN-13: 978-1-935077-41-1 (pbk.)
  ISBN-10: 1-935077-41-4 (pbk.)
  1. Marsh ecology--Georgia--Juvenile literature. 2. Marsh animals--Georgia--Juvenile literature. 3. Swamp ecology--Georgia--Juvenile literature. 4. Swamp animals--Georgia--Juvenile literature. I. Title.
  QH105.G4B4645 2009
  577.6809758--dc22

                  2009012571

Table of Contents

Grasses grow in a salt marsh.

Grasses and cattails grow in a freshwater marsh.

Mountains

Piedmont

Coastal Plain

Marsh and Swamp

Coast

Okefenokee Swamp

Atlantic Ocean

Trees and woody plants grow in the swamp.

What's the Difference Between a Marsh and a Swamp?

Smooth cordgrass sways in the ocean breeze. Farther inland, an alligator slides into the water of the wetland **habitat**. Wetlands are areas of land covered with water all or part of the time. Marshes and swamps are wetland habitats. A habitat is a place where plants and animals live. What's the difference in these habitats? It's the plants! Trees and other woody bushes grow in a swamp. Grasses grow in a marsh.

Saltwater marshes lie along the Georgia coast. Freshwater marshes lie further inland. Grasses and cattails grow here. Alligators, frogs, and turtles live here. Many kinds of fish swim in the fresh water.

A great egret wades
across the trembling earth.

The swamp has fields of
grass and water lilies
called prairies.

The Cypress tree's knobby knees stick out of the water.

The Okefenokee Swamp

The Okefenokee Swamp is one of the largest swamps in the United States. New plants grow on top of **decayed**, or dead, plant layers under the water. These layers are called **peat**. They form floating islands. These islands can vibrate when someone walks on them. The Indians called the Okefenokee *trembling earth*. Acid from the peat makes the water look dark. But it's not dirty!

Cypress trees grow in the swampy water. Their trunks are thick at the base. It helps to hold them up. They have knobby roots that stick out of the water. These roots are called **knees**. The Okefenokee has large, watery fields of grass and water lilies. These fields are called **prairies**.

Raccoon

Osprey

Whitetail Deer

Armadillo

Gray Fox

Bobcat

Black Bear

Many animals live on the land.

8

Animals and Birds on the Land

The swamp is a crowded place. Black bears and whitetail deer live here. Wild pigs and bobcats live here. So does the gray fox. Raccoons, opossums, and armadillos prowl around at night.

Sandhill cranes nest in open areas away from trees. Ospreys build their nests high in trees near the grassy prairies.

It's a Fact!

Sandhill cranes are the watchmen of the swamp. They trumpet when they are startled. The cry can be heard for miles. Other cranes recognize the distress signal. They take up the call. They all fly away.

Beaver

Anhinga

River Otter

Chain
Pickerel

Florida
Cooter
Turtle

Cottonmouth
(Water Moccasin)

Other animals live in or near the water.

Animals and Fish in the Water

Alligators hunt for snakes, fish, and turtles to eat. Beavers and river otters work and play in the water. Bowfin and chain pickerel swim below.

Anhingas look like turkeys with webbed feet. They are even called *water turkey* by many people. They can fly. They can swim on top of the water. They can dive in and swim very fast under the water.

Frogs and salamanders depend on wetlands to survive. They are very sensitive to air and water pollution. Some are dying because of this.

Alligator

Sundew

Bladderwort

Pitcher Plant

Some plants eat insects!

Plants that Eat Animals!

Carnivorous plants eat animals! Pitcher plants hold water in their leaves. Insects crawl to the edge and fall in. Stiff hairs near the top won't let them crawl out again.

Bladderworts float on the water. They have small **bladders** below the water. The bladder holds air. It opens when tiny insects and water creatures swim by. It sucks them in. Once inside, these creatures are trapped!

Sundew has a sticky substance on its leaves. Gnats and small insects come to taste, but they can't get away. They're stuck!

Smooth cordgrass has adapted to the salty water.

There are saltwater marshes all along the Georgia coast.

The water level falls when the tide goes out.

Saltwater Marshes Along Georgia's Coast

The saltwater marshes are along the coast of Georgia. The marsh is a hard place to live because of the **tide**. The tide is the rising and falling of the water levels of the ocean. When the tide rises, the water level goes up. The marsh becomes saltier. The temperature of the water changes. When the tide falls, the water level goes down. In some places, the ground can be seen. Plants and animals must **adapt** to these constant changes. They must change their behavior to live.

Most plants die when they are flooded by saltwater. But not smooth cordgrass. It covers the marsh. It has adapted to living here. Its roots and leaves actually remove salt from water the plant needs to live.

Oyster Bed

The tide carries nutrients through the estuary and marsh. Grasses and other organisms like mud oysters and fiddler crabs feed on this.

Small Fish

Nutrients from the marsh go back into the estuaries to feed oysters, small fish, and other organisms.

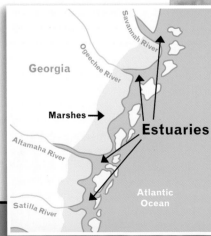

Savannah River

Ogeechee River

Georgia

Marshes →

Estuaries

Altamaha River

Satilla River

Atlantic Ocean

Fiddler Crabs

Estuaries are places where fresh water from rivers and creeks meets salt water from the ocean.

From Ocean to Marsh and Back Again

Estuaries lie between the salt marshes and the ocean. These are places where fresh water from rivers and creeks mixes with salt water from the ocean.

The ocean tide brings **nutrients** from the estuaries into the marshes. Nutrients also come into the marshes from the rivers and creeks. These nutrients are the food and chemicals that **organisms** need to live and grow. Organisms are living things. When the tide falls, it carries decayed marsh plants and animal waste back into the estuaries. This becomes food for organisms that live there. The tide also helps clean the marshes. It removes dead grass and other waste.

Mosquito

Great Blue Heron

Clapper Rail

Marsh Rabbit

Diamond Back Terrapin

Snowy Egret

Great blue herons and snowy egrets wander in looking for food.

Animals and Birds in the Marsh

Mosquitoes, midges, and deerflies annoy any humans who go into the salt marsh. Snails live in the mud. Alligators wander into the shallow water to eat. But they don't like salt water. They live in the freshwater marshes upstream.

Clapper rails and seaside sparrows nest in the salt marsh. Great blue herons and snowy egrets wade in the marsh at low tide looking for food.

Diamond back terrapins are the only turtles that live in the salt water marsh. Raccoons and marsh rabbits hunt for food in the cordgrass.

It's a Fact!

The periwinkle snail can spend its entire life on one blade of grass.

Shrimp

Clams

Mussels

Oysters
are good
to eat!

Oysters

Seafood grows in the marshes and estuaries.

Seafood in the Marsh and Estuary

Oysters, mussels, and clams live in the estuaries. The salt marshes and estuaries are also **nurseries**! They protect many young animals while they grow. Young blue crabs, shrimp, and fish come into the estuaries from the ocean. The marsh and estuary habitat protects them from **predators**. Predators hunt other animals for food. When the young animals are adults, they swim back to the ocean. Without the salt marshes and estuaries, we wouldn't have seafood to eat!

Blue Crab

Glossary

adapt – Changes in behavior that an animal or plant makes to live or survive.

bladder – An underwater air sac that is part of a plant like bladderwort.

carnivorous plants – Plants that eat insects and other tiny animals.

decayed – Dead plant or animal material.

estuary – A place where fresh water from rivers and creeks mixes with salt water from the ocean.

habitat – A place where plants and animals live naturally.

knees – The knobby roots of a cypress tree.

nurseries – Safe places for young animals to grow.

nutrients – Food and chemicals that living things need to live and grow.

organisms – Living things.

peat – Layers of decayed plants in a swamp.

prairies – Watery fields of grass and water lilies found in a swamp.

predators – Animals that hunt other animals for food.

tide – The rising and falling of the water levels of the ocean.

Word Index

Image Credits

About the Author

Doraine Bennett has a degree in professional writing from Columbus State University in Columbus, Georgia, and has been writing and teaching writing for over twenty years. She has authored numerous articles in magazines for both children and adults and is the editor of the National Infantry Association's *Infantry Bugler* magazine. Doraine enjoys reading and writing books and articles for children. She lives in Georgia with her husband, Cliff.